frame >by >frame
quick & easy

frame >by >frame
quick & easy

the cookbook that shows you every step

First published in 2009
Love Food ® is an imprint of Parragon Books Ltd

Parragon
Queen Street House
4 Queen Street
Bath BA1 1HE, UK

ISBN: 978-1-4075-7804-0

Printed in China

Designed by Talking Design
Photography by Mike Cooper
Food styling by Lincoln Jefferson
New recipes by Christine France
Introduction by Linda Doeser

Notes for the Reader

This book uses both metric and imperial measurements. Follow the same units of measurement throughout; do not mix metric and imperial. All spoon measurements are level: teaspoons are assumed to be 5 ml, and tablespoons are assumed to be 15 ml. Unless otherwise stated, milk is assumed to be full fat, eggs and individual vegetables are medium, and pepper is freshly ground black pepper.

The times given are an approximate guide only. Preparation times differ according to the techniques used by different people and the cooking times may also vary from those given. Optional ingredients, variations or serving suggestions have not been included in the calculations.

Recipes using raw or very lightly cooked eggs should be avoided by infants, the elderly, pregnant women, convalescents and anyone suffering from an illness. Pregnant and breastfeeding women are advised to avoid eating peanuts and peanut products. Sufferers from nut allergies should be aware that some of the ready-made ingredients used in the recipes in this book may contain nuts. Always check the packaging before use. Vegetarians should be aware that some brands of the ready-made ingredients used in the recipes in this book may contain animal products. Always check the packaging before use.

contents

introduction

This superb cookbook with its wealth of beautiful and immensely useful photographs will prove to be an invaluable addition to any cook's bookshelf. The recipes are clear, easy to follow, beautifully illustrated and temptingly tasty, so whatever your level of expertise in the kitchen you are virtually guaranteed success every time.

Every recipe starts with a photograph of all the ingredients but this is more than just a pretty picture or – even less helpful – a montage that is not to scale so that a chilli appears to be the same size as a whole fish. Instead, it serves as a handy way of checking that you have everything ready before you start cooking. Just comparing the picture with the ingredients arranged on your own worktop or kitchen table will ensure that you haven't missed anything out and when it's time to add the garlic, for example, you have already chopped it as specified in the ingredients list. If you're uncertain about how small to dice fruit or how finely to crush biscuits, a glance at the photograph will provide an instant answer.

Each short and straightforward step of the method is clearly explained without any jargon or difficult technical terms. Once again, what you see in the photograph is what you should expect to see in front of you. Not only is this reassuring for the novice cook, those with more experience will find it a helpful reminder of the little touches that can easily be overlooked. Each recipe ends with a lovely photograph of the finished dish, complete with any serving suggestions.

Why you need this book

Eating well is one of the primary keys to good health for you and your family, yet the pace of modern life is often frantic and time is limited.

No one really wants or can afford to spend hours in the kitchen and, equally important, no one wants to struggle trying to understand a complicated recipe that somehow always turns out to be disappointing and not at all what they expected.

In this book there are over 50 fuss-free recipes for delicious dishes for all occasions and every taste, from succulent stir-fried beef to elegant glazed duck and from spicy seafood stew to great vegetarian grills and bakes, as well as wonderfully self-indulgent desserts. All of them take less than half an hour to prepare and many can be made in just minutes.

top tips for quick and easy cooking

* Read all the way through the recipe – ingredients list and method – before you start so that you know exactly what you will need. Scrabbling about at the back of the storecupboard to find a rarely used ingredient or moving half a dozen other utensils to reach the one you need in the middle of cooking a dish is, at best, exasperating and, at worst, liable to cause the dish you are cooking to burn.

* Ovens and grills take time to heat up so, if you are going to use either of them, turn them on as soon as you go into the kitchen. Fan-assisted ovens do not usually require preheating, but conventional ovens can take 15 minutes to reach the specified temperature. If the recipe calls for boiling water, switch the kettle on in advance.

* Collect all your ingredients together and make sure that they are ready to use – vegetables peeled or washed, for example. In addition, do any initial preparation described in the ingredients list, such as chopping onions. Check with the photograph.

* Arrange the plates and bowls of ingredients in the order in which they are to be used. If a number of ingredients, such as flavourings and spices, are to be added at the same time, put them in small piles on the same plate.

* As you finish using utensils, move them out of your way. A cluttered worktop is the enemy of speed and efficiency and can be dangerous.

* Be realistic about how much time you have and what you can you reasonably handle. It's no good cooking the main course in a flash if the vegetables you intended to accompany it are going to take a lot longer. Consider a no-cook dessert or a starter that can be prepared in advance if the main course requires your undivided attention.

* Take advantage of convenience foods, such as bags of diced vegetables, trimmed and washed leeks, ready-made pesto, canned pulses and tomatoes, and jars of ready-chopped garlic, ginger and chillies. These will be more expensive than ingredients you have to prepare yourself, so strike a balance between cost and saving time. Remember that some convenience foods come at the price of flavour and are not really worth buying.

time-saving shortcuts

* Not all vegetables, including potatoes, have to be peeled before cooking. Most of the nutrients are often found just under the skin, so it is better to simply scrub them. After cooking, they can be peeled if necessary, or, if very young, they can be served 'in their jackets'. Thin-skinned vegetables, such as courgettes and aubergines, do not need peeling at all. 'Old' vegetables do need to be peeled and so too do carrots, even young ones, because they have a tendency to retain agricultural chemicals just beneath the skin.

* The easiest way to peel tomatoes, nectarines, peaches and shallots is to put them into a heatproof bowl and pour in boiling water to cover. Leave to stand for 30–60 seconds and drain. The skins will slip off much more easily. Tomatoes and peaches will be even easier to peel if you slit the skins first.

* To peel a garlic clove, lightly crush it by pressing down with the flat blade of a cook's knife. The skin can then be removed easily and the garlic can be chopped, sliced or, quickest of all, crushed with a garlic press.

* Some ingredients – ham, bacon, some fresh herbs and dried fruit, for example – are much easier and quicker to snip into pieces with scissors rather than dice with a knife. Trim green beans and mangetouts with kitchen scissors too.

* Don't bother to peel avocados if you're going to mash or process the flesh. Simply halve and stone, then scoop out the flesh with a teaspoon.

* To coat cubes of meat in flour before browning, put the flour into a polythene bag and add the cubes a few at a time. Hold the bag closed and shake gently until the meat is coated. Repeat until finished.

* When slicing soft cheese, such as Camembert, dampen the blade of the knife to prevent the slices from sticking.

* To deseed peppers, halve them lengthways and cut out the membranes, together with most of the seeds, with a small knife. Turn the halves over and tap sharply on a chopping board so that any remaining seeds fall out.

* Melt chocolate in the microwave oven. Break it into pieces and put it into a microwave-proof bowl. Heat on MEDIUM for 10 seconds, then stir. Return to the microwave and heat for another 10 seconds before checking and stirring again – even when it's melted it will hold its shape so you cannot tell if it's ready just by looking at it. White chocolate should be heated on LOW.

* If you have any leftover fresh breadcrumbs or grated cheese, divide into portions and freeze for another day. They make the perfect quick topping for gratins or bakes.

* Leftover wine can also be frozen. Freeze it in an ice-cube tray and the next time you're cooking a casserole you can pop in a cube or two to add extra flavour.

* When you are using the food processor to chop vegetables, such as onions, make extra and store in sealed polythene bags in the refrigerator, ready to use as and when you need them during the week.

useful equipment

✳ **Wok:** Stir-frying is one of the fastest techniques for cooking food. The principle is simple: ingredients are cut, sliced or chopped into small, even-sized pieces and then stirred over a very high heat in a small amount of oil for a brief period until cooked through and tender.

A wok is basically a gently sloping conical pan designed for constant stirring so that food moves continually back to the centre where the heat is the most intense. Woks with a round base work well on gas hobs, while flat-based woks are designed for electric and ceramic hobs. Some models have two ear-shaped handles, while others have a long wooden handle, sometimes combined with a short opposite handle that makes it easy to lift the pan. The most useful woks are made from heavy carbon steel which distributes the heat quickly and evenly. Stainless steel woks tend to scorch and many non-stick woks cannot withstand the high temperature required for stir-frying. A new wok usually needs to be seasoned with oil and heated to create a natural non-stick patina: follow the manufacturer's instructions. A wok with a diameter of 35 cm/14 inches is ideal for most family meals and one with a lid is more versatile.

✳ **Saucepans:** It is worth buying a selection of different-sized pans with thick, flat bases and tight-fitting lids. It is also sensible to ensure that handles, including those on lids, are heatproof

and, if you are left-handed, that you can pour liquids and sauces safely and easily. The size of the pan directly affects the efficiency of the cooking. If it is too small, it is difficult to stir a dish and liquids can boil over. Some ingredients may be cooked through while others are still almost raw. If the pan is too large, again the cooking may not be even and will take longer – you are also wasting heat. Non-stick linings are a matter of personal choice.

✳ **Frying pan:** A large (23–28-cm/9–11-inch) heavy-based frying pan with gently sloping sides is invaluable for softening onions, browning meat and so on. If it has a heatproof handle, it can also be used under the grill or even in the oven. A smaller pan is ideal for dry-frying spices, seeds and nuts and cooking omelettes. Non-stick pans produce healthier meals since they reduce the amount of oil required, and they are very easy to clean.

* **Griddle pan:** This may be either flat or ridged and is usually made of cast iron for even distribution of heat. It is designed to be used over high, fast-cooking heat. Ridged pans prevent the ingredients from soaking in oil or fat, and will give the food you're cooking those characteristic charred lines.

* **Steamer:** Steaming is an economical and healthy way of cooking with the food placed in a perforated container over a boiling liquid – water, stock or wine. The simplest way to do this is to stand a basin on top of a grooved trivet in the base of a saucepan partly filled with simmering water. A tiered, stacking steel steamer is more versatile, allowing you to stew a dish in the bottom container while steaming vegetables above. A fold-out, tulip-shaped steamer, available in two sizes, fits almost any size of saucepan but its central stalk slightly limits the quantity of ingredients you can steam. A universal steamer has a round, firm, perforated, stepped base that will fit on top of any saucepan. It is an extremely useful utensil. Stacking bamboo steamers with lids are usually used in a wok. Soak them well in cold water before using for the first time. If you find that you like the taste of steamed food, you may want to invest in an electric food steamer. These have separate tiers or compartments for cooking different foods, and can be fully dismantled for easy cleaning.

* **Knives:** Good-quality, heavy knives are essential to any kitchen – cook's, utility, paring and vegetable knives are the minimum requirement. Before buying, check that the weight of the knife is evenly balanced and that the handle feels comfortable. Store them in a knife block and treat them with care, keeping them well sharpened with a V-sharpener, carborundum stone or steel. Sharp knives are both more efficient and safer because they are less likely to slip.

* **Vegetable peeler:** The all-metal, swivel-blade peeler is the best known type and very easy to use. It peels thinly and is suitable for both left- and right-handed cooks. The Y-shaped peeler also has a swivel blade and a sturdy handle that is easy to grasp. Besides peeling fruit and vegetables, these inexpensive tools are good for de-stringing celery and rhubarb, and shaving chocolate and hard cheeses, such as Parmesan.

* **Hand-held blender:** Also known as a stick blender, this useful and inexpensive tool is invaluable for whisking soups and sauces while they are still in the saucepan – a great time-saver.

* **Food processor:** Although this is an expensive piece of equipment that is bulky enough to cause storage problems in a small kitchen, it can, nevertheless, be a great time-saver and will take the hard work out of many jobs in the kitchen. Besides reducing mixtures to a purée, a food processor can be used for chopping, slicing, grinding, beating, whisking and making breadcrumbs. For durability, choose a model with a powerful motor.

vegetarian

falafel
burgers

serves 4

ingredients
800 g/1 lb 12 oz canned
  chickpeas, drained
1 small onion, chopped
grated rind and juice of
  1 lime
2 tsp ground coriander
2 tsp ground cumin
6 tbsp plain flour
4 tbsp olive oil
salt and pepper
4 sprigs fresh basil, to garnish
tomato salsa, to serve

> **>1** Put the chickpeas, onion, lime rind and juice and the spices into a food processor and process to a coarse paste. Season to taste with salt and pepper.

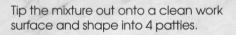

> **>2** Tip the mixture out onto a clean work surface and shape into 4 patties.

Garnish with basil sprigs and
serve with tomato salsa.

> 3 Spread out the flour on a large plate and
use to coat the patties.

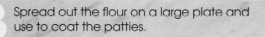

> 4 Heat the oil in a large frying pan, add the
burgers and cook over a medium heat for
2 minutes on each side, or until crisp.

mushroom polenta grill

serves 4

ingredients

250-g/9-oz block ready-made
  polenta
4 large portobello mushrooms
60 g/2¼ oz butter

1 garlic clove, crushed
1 tbsp chopped fresh parsley
1 tbsp snipped fresh chives, plus
  extra to garnish
4 very fresh eggs

100 g/3½ oz baby spinach
  leaves
salt and pepper
Parmesan cheese shavings,
  to serve

> **1** Preheat the grill to high. Cut the polenta into 8 slices and arrange on a foil-lined grill rack with the mushrooms.

> **2** Melt the butter in a small pan with the garlic. Stir in the parsley and chives.

> **3** Brush the mushrooms and polenta with the herb butter and season to taste with salt and pepper.

> **4** Cook under the preheated grill for 6–8 minutes, turning once, until the polenta is golden and mushrooms are tender.

>5 Bring a pan of water to just under boiling point. Break the eggs carefully into the water.

>6 Poach the eggs for about 3 minutes, until just set. Lift out with a slotted spoon.

>7 Place two slices of polenta on each serving plate and add a small handful of spinach leaves.

>8 Top each with a mushroom, then add a poached egg and spoon over the remaining herb butter.

Sprinkle with Parmesan shavings to serve
and garnish with chives.

jamaican rice & peas with tofu

serves 4

ingredients

250 g/9 oz firm tofu
2 tbsp chopped fresh thyme,
  plus extra sprigs to garnish

2 tbsp olive oil
1 onion, sliced
1 garlic clove, crushed
1 small fresh red chilli, chopped

400 ml/14 fl oz vegetable stock
200 g/7 oz basmati rice
4 tbsp coconut cream

400 g/14 oz canned red kidney
  beans, drained
salt and pepper

>**1** Cut the tofu into bite-sized cubes. Toss with half the chopped thyme and sprinkle with salt and pepper to taste.

>**2** Heat 1 tablespoon of the oil in a frying pan and fry the tofu, stirring occasionally, for 2 minutes. Remove and keep warm.

>**3** Fry the onion in the remaining oil, stirring, for 3–4 minutes.

>**4** Stir in the garlic, chilli and the remaining chopped thyme, then add the stock and bring to the boil.

>5 Stir in the rice, then reduce the heat, cover and simmer for 12–15 minutes, until the rice is tender.

>6 Stir in the coconut cream and beans, season to taste with salt and pepper and cook gently for 2–3 minutes.

Spoon the tofu over the rice and serve hot,
garnished with thyme sprigs.

grilled halloumi skewers on fennel & white bean salad

serves 4

ingredients

200 g/7 oz halloumi cheese
1 garlic clove, crushed
1 fennel bulb, thinly sliced
1 small red onion, thinly sliced
400 g/14 oz canned cannellini
  beans, drained
balsamic vinegar, to serve

dressing

finely grated rind and juice
  of 1 lemon
3 tbsp chopped fresh
  flat-leaf parsley
4 tbsp olive oil
salt and pepper

>1 For the dressing, mix together the lemon rind and juice, parsley and oil with salt and pepper to taste.

>2 Cut the halloumi into 2-cm/¾-inch cubes, thread onto four pre-soaked wooden skewers and brush with half the dressing.

Serve the skewers with the salad, sprinkled with a little balsamic vinegar.

>3 Preheat the grill to high. Cook the skewers under the preheated grill for 6–8 minutes, turning once, until golden.

>4 Heat the remaining dressing and the garlic in a small pan until boiling. Combine with the fennel, onion and beans.

risotto with asparagus & walnuts

serves 4

ingredients

15 g/½ oz butter
3 tbsp olive oil
1 small onion, finely chopped

350 g/12 oz risotto rice
150 ml/5 fl oz dry white wine
1.5 litres/2¾ pints hot vegetable
  stock

200 g/7 oz asparagus tips,
  cut into 6-cm/2½-inch lengths
40 g/1½ oz chopped walnuts
grated rind of 1 lemon

salt and pepper
walnut oil, to serve (optional)
strips of lemon zest, to garnish

> 1 Heat the butter and olive oil in a large saucepan and fry the onion, stirring, for 3–4 minutes, until softened.

> 2 Add the rice and stir over a medium heat for 1 minute, without browning.

> 3 Add the wine and boil rapidly, stirring, until almost all evaporated.

> 4 Stir the stock into the pan a ladleful at a time, allowing each ladleful to be absorbed before adding more.

>5 After 10 minutes, add the asparagus and continue cooking, adding stock when necessary.

>6 After a further 5 minutes, test a grain of rice – it should be 'al dente' or firm to the bite.

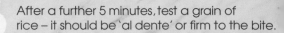

>7 Stir in the walnuts and lemon rind, then adjust the seasoning, adding salt and pepper to taste.

>8 Remove from the heat and drizzle over a little walnut oil, if using, stirring in lightly.

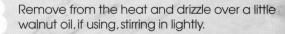

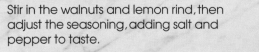

Serve the risotto immediately, garnished
with strips of lemon zest.

tacos with chickpea salsa

serves 4

ingredients
2 firm, ripe avocados
1 tbsp lime juice
1 tomato, diced
1 tbsp olive oil

1 small onion, sliced
400 g/14 oz canned chickpeas,
 drained
1 tsp mild chilli powder
8 Cos lettuce leaves

8 tacos
2 tbsp chopped fresh
 coriander, plus extra sprigs
 to garnish
salt and pepper

150 ml/5 fl oz soured cream,
 to serve

>1 Halve, stone, peel and dice the avocados and toss with the lime juice.

>2 Stir in the tomato and season well with salt and pepper.

>3 Heat the oil in a saucepan and fry the onion for 3–4 minutes, or until golden brown.

>4 Mash the chickpeas with a fork and stir into the pan with the chilli powder. Heat gently, stirring, for 2 minutes.

5 Divide the lettuce between the tacos. Stir the chopped coriander into the avocado and tomato mixture, then spoon into the tacos.

>**6** Add a spoonful of the chickpea mixture to each taco and top with a spoonful of soured cream.

Garnish with coriander sprigs and serve immediately.

courgette, carrot & tomato frittata

serves 2–4

ingredients
1 tsp olive oil
1 onion, cut into
  small wedges
1–2 garlic cloves, crushed
2 eggs
2 egg whites
1 courgette, trimmed
  and grated
2 carrots, peeled
  and grated
2 tomatoes, chopped
pepper
1 tbsp shredded
  fresh basil, to garnish

> **1** Heat the oil in a large non-stick frying pan, add the onion and garlic and sauté for 5 minutes, stirring frequently.

> **2** Beat together the eggs and egg whites in a bowl, then pour into the pan.

Sprinkle with the shredded basil, cut the frittata into quarters and serve.

> 3 Using a spatula, pull the egg mixture from the sides of the pan into the centre, allowing the uncooked egg to run underneath.

> 4 When the base has set lightly, add the courgette, carrots and tomatoes. Season to taste with pepper and continue to cook over a low heat until the eggs are cooked to your liking.

tofu stir-fry

serves 4

ingredients

2 tbsp sunflower oil

350 g/12 oz firm tofu, cubed

225 g/8 oz pak choi, roughly chopped

1 garlic clove, chopped

4 tbsp sweet chilli sauce

2 tbsp light soy sauce

>1 Heat 1 tablespoon of the oil in a wok.

>2 Add the tofu to the wok in batches and stir-fry for 2–3 minutes, until golden. Remove and set aside.

>3 Add the pak choi to the wok and stir-fry for a few seconds, until tender and wilted. Remove and set aside.

>4 Heat the remaining oil in the wok, then add the garlic and stir-fry for 30 seconds.

>5 Stir in the chilli sauce and soy sauce and bring to the boil.

>6 Return the tofu and pak choi to the wok and toss gently until coated in the sauce.

Transfer to individual dishes and serve immediately.

fusilli with courgettes & lemon

serves 4

ingredients

6 tbsp olive oil
1 small onion, very thinly sliced
2 garlic cloves, very finely
  chopped

2 tbsp chopped fresh rosemary
1 tbsp chopped fresh flat-leaf
  parsley
450 g/1 lb small courgettes,
  cut into 4-cm/1½-inch strips

finely grated rind of 1 lemon
450 g/1 lb dried fusilli
salt and pepper
4 tbsp freshly grated Parmesan
  cheese, to serve

>1 Heat the oil in a large frying pan over a low–medium heat. Add the onion and cook gently, stirring occasionally, for about 10 minutes, until golden.

>2 Increase the heat to medium–high. Add the garlic, rosemary and parsley. Cook for a few seconds, stirring.

>3 Add the courgettes and lemon rind. Cook for 5–7 minutes, stirring occasionally, until just tender. Season to taste with salt and pepper. Remove from the heat.

>4 Bring a large saucepan of lightly salted water to the boil. Add the pasta, bring back to the boil and cook for 8–10 minutes, or until tender but still firm to the bite.

>5 Drain the pasta and transfer to a warmed serving dish.

>6 Briefly reheat the courgette sauce. Pour over the pasta and toss well to mix.

Sprinkle with the Parmesan cheese and serve immediately.

double cheese macaroni

serves 4

ingredients

225 g/8 oz dried macaroni
250 g/9 oz ricotta cheese
1½ tbsp wholegrain mustard
3 tbsp snipped fresh chives,
  plus extra to garnish
200 g/7 oz cherry tomatoes,
  halved
100 g/3½ oz sun-dried
  tomatoes in oil, drained
  and chopped
butter or oil, for greasing
100 g/3½ oz Cheddar cheese,
  grated
salt and pepper

>1 Bring a large saucepan of lightly salted water to the boil. Add the pasta and cook for 10–12 minutes, or until tender but still firm to the bite. Drain.

>2 Mix the ricotta with the mustard, chives and salt and pepper to taste. Stir in the macaroni, cherry tomatoes and sun-dried tomatoes.

Serve the macaroni sprinkled with extra chives.

>**3** Grease a 1.7-litre/3-pint shallow ovenproof dish. Spoon in the macaroni mixture, spreading evenly.

>**4** Preheat the grill to high. Sprinkle the Cheddar cheese over the macaroni mixture and cook under the preheated grill for 4–5 minutes, until golden and bubbling.

goat's cheese tarts
makes about 12

ingredients
melted butter, for greasing
400 g/14 oz ready-rolled puff
  pastry

flour, for dusting
1 egg, beaten
about 3 tbsp onion relish or
  tomato relish

350 g/12 oz goat's cheese logs,
  sliced into rounds
olive oil, for drizzling
pepper

>1 Preheat the oven to 200°C/400°F/Gas Mark 6. Grease 1–2 baking trays with melted butter.

>2 Transfer the pastry sheet to a lightly floured work surface and roll out lightly to remove any creases, if necessary.

>3 Use a 7.5-cm/3-inch pastry cutter to stamp out as many rounds as possible.

>4 Place the rounds on the baking trays and press gently about 2.5 cm/1 inch from the edge of each with a 5-cm/2-inch pastry cutter.

49

Brush the rounds with the beaten egg and prick with a fork.

Top each round with a teaspoon of the relish and a slice of the goat's cheese.

>7

Drizzle with oil and sprinkle over a little pepper.

>8

Bake in the preheated oven for 8–10 minutes, until the pastry is crisp and the cheese is bubb

Serve warm.

mushroom & cauliflower cheese crumble

serves 4

ingredients
1 cauliflower, cut into florets
55 g/2 oz butter

115 g/4 oz button mushrooms,
  sliced
salt and pepper

topping
115 g/4 oz dry breadcrumbs
2 tbsp grated Parmesan
  cheese

1 tsp dried oregano
1 tsp dried parsley
25 g/1 oz butter

> **1** Bring a large saucepan of lightly salted water to the boil. Add the cauliflower and cook for 3 minutes.

> **2** Remove from the heat, drain well and transfer to a shallow ovenproof dish.

> **3** Preheat the oven to 230°C/450°F/ Gas Mark 8. Melt the butter in a small frying pan over a medium heat. Add the mushrooms, stir and cook gently for 3 minutes.

> **4** Remove from the heat and spoon on top of the cauliflower. Season to taste with salt and pepper.

53

>5 Combine the breadcrumbs, Parmesan and herbs in a small mixing bowl, then sprinkle over the vegetables.

>6 Dice the butter and dot over the breadcrumb mixture. Bake in the preheated oven for 15 minutes, or until the topping is golden brown.

Serve straight from the cooking dish.

tomato ratatouille

serves 4

ingredients

1 tsp olive oil
1 onion, cut into small wedges
2–4 garlic cloves, chopped
1 small aubergine, chopped
1 red and 1 yellow pepper,
   deseeded and chopped
1 courgette, chopped
2 tbsp tomato purée
3 tbsp water
115 g/4 oz mushrooms, halved
225 g/8 oz tomatoes, chopped
pepper
1 tbsp shredded fresh basil,
   to garnish
2 tbsp grated Parmesan
   cheese, to serve

> **1** Heat the oil in a heavy-based saucepan. Add the onion, garlic and aubergine and cook, stirring frequently, for 3 minutes.

> **2** Add the red and yellow peppers and the courgette.

Divide the ratatouille between warmed dishes, garnish with shredded basil and serve with Parmesan cheese.

>3 Mix together the tomato purée and water in a small bowl and stir into the pan. Bring to the boil, cover, reduce the heat to a simmer and cook for 10 minutes.

>4 Add the mushrooms and tomatoes, with pepper to taste, and continue to simmer for 12–15 minutes, stirring occasionally, until the vegetables are tender.

fish

monkfish with a lemon & parsley crust

serves 4

ingredients

4 tbsp sunflower oil
4 tbsp fresh breadcrumbs
4 tbsp chopped fresh parsley,
  plus extra sprigs to garnish
finely grated rind of 1 large
  lemon
4 monkfish fillets, about
  140–175 g/5–6 oz each
salt and pepper

>1 Preheat the oven to 180°C/350°F/
Gas Mark 4. Mix together the oil,
breadcrumbs, parsley and lemon
rind in a bowl until well combined.
Season to taste with salt and pepper.

>2 Place the fish fillets in a large roasting tin.

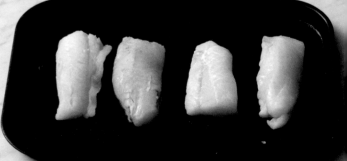

Garnish with parsley sprigs and serve.

> **3** Divide the breadcrumb mixture between the fish and press it down with your fingers to ensure it covers the fillets.

> **4** Bake in the preheated oven for 7–8 minutes, or until the fish is cooked through.

quick & creamy fish pie

serves 4

ingredients

1 tbsp olive oil
2 shallots, finely chopped
150 ml/5 fl oz dry white wine or
 fish stock
1 bay leaf

200 g/7 oz closed cup
 mushrooms, thickly sliced
100 g/3½ oz crème fraîche
500 g/1 lb 2 oz firm white fish
 fillets, cut into chunks

175 g/6 oz cooked peeled
 prawns
175 g/6 oz frozen peas
40 g/1½ oz butter, melted
150 g/5½ oz fresh white
 breadcrumbs

salt and pepper
chopped fresh parsley,
 to garnish

>1 Heat the oil in an ovenproof saucepan or a shallow flameproof casserole and fry the shallots for 2–3 minutes, until softened.

>2 Add the wine, bay leaf and mushrooms and simmer for 2 minutes, stirring occasionally.

>3 Stir in the crème fraîche and add the fish. Season to taste with salt and pepper.

>4 Bring to the boil, cover and simmer for 5–6 minutes, until the fish is almost cooked.

>**5** Remove and discard the bay leaf, then add the prawns and peas and bring back to the boil.

>**6** Meanwhile, re-melt the butter in a separate saucepan, if necessary, and stir in the breadcrumbs. Preheat the grill to medium.

>**7** Spread the breadcrumb mixture evenly over the top of the fish mixture.

>**8** Place the saucepan under the preheated grill for 3–4 minutes, until the topping is golden brown and bubbling.

Sprinkle with fresh parsley and serve hot.

thai prawn noodle bowl

serves 4

ingredients

1 bunch spring onions
2 celery sticks
1 red pepper
200 g/7 oz rice vermicelli
  noodles

2 tbsp groundnut oil
55 g/2 oz unsalted peanuts
1 fresh bird's eye chilli, sliced
1 lemon grass stem, crushed
400 ml/14 fl oz fish or chicken
  stock

200 ml/7 fl oz coconut milk
2 tsp Thai fish sauce
350 g/12 oz cooked peeled
  king prawns
salt and pepper

3 tbsp chopped fresh
  coriander, to garnish

Trim the spring onions and celery and thinly slice diagonally. Deseed and thinly slice the pepper.

Place the noodles in a bowl, cover with boiling water and leave to stand for 4 minutes, or until tender. Drain.

Heat the oil in a wok and stir-fry the peanuts for 1–2 minutes, until golden. Lift out with a slotted spoon.

Add the sliced vegetables to the wok and stir-fry over a high heat for 1–2 minutes.

>5 Add the chilli, lemon grass, stock, coconut milk and fish sauce and bring to the boil.

>6 Stir in the prawns and bring back to the boil, stirring. Season to taste with salt and pepper, then add the noodles.

Serve in warmed bowls, sprinkled with fresh coriander.

peppered tuna steaks

serves 4

ingredients

4 tuna steaks, about 175 g/
  6 oz each
4 tsp sunflower oil or olive oil
1 tsp salt
2 tbsp pink, green and black
  peppercorns, roughly crushed
handful of fresh rocket leaves,
  to garnish
lemon wedges, to serve

>1 Brush the tuna steaks with the oil.

>2 Sprinkle with the salt.

Garnish with rocket and serve with lemon wedges for squeezing over.

>3 Coat the fish in the crushed peppercorns.

>4 Heat a ridged griddle pan over a medium heat. Add the tuna and cook for 2–3 minutes on each side.

sea bass with olive gremolata

serves 4

ingredients
900 g/2 lb small new potatoes
4 sea bass fillets, about
  175 g/6 oz each
1 tbsp olive oil

4 tbsp dry white wine
salt and pepper

olive gremolata
grated rind of 1 lemon
1 garlic clove, chopped
2 large handfuls flat-leaf
  parsley (about 55 g/2 oz)

70 g/2½ oz stoned black olives
2 tbsp capers
2 tbsp olive oil

>1 Cook the potatoes in a saucepan of lightly salted boiling water for 15–20 minutes, or until tender.

>2 Meanwhile, make the gremolata. Place the lemon rind, garlic, parsley, olives, capers and oil in a food processor and process briefly to form a rough paste.

>3 Brush the sea bass with the oil and season to taste with salt and pepper. Heat a heavy-based frying pan and fry the sea bass for 5–6 minutes, turning once.

>4 Remove the fish from the pan and keep warm. Stir the wine into the pan and boil for 1 minute, stirring.

>5 Add the gremolata to the pan and stir for a few seconds to heat gently.

>6 Drain the potatoes when tender and crush lightly with a wooden spoon or potato masher.

Serve the sea bass and crushed potatoes topped with the gremolata.

fish goujons with chilli mayonnaise

serves 4

ingredients
200 g/7 oz plain flour
3 eggs
140 g/5 oz matzo meal or
   crushed crackers

450 g/1 lb firm white fish fillets,
   cut into strips
sunflower or groundnut oil,
   for shallow-frying
salt and pepper

chilli mayonnaise
2 tbsp sweet chilli sauce
4–5 tbsp mayonnaise

> **1** Mix the flour with plenty of salt and pepper on a large flat plate.

> **2** Beat the eggs in a bowl.

> **3** Spread out the matzo meal on another flat plate.

> **4** Dip the fish pieces into the seasoned flour, then into the beaten egg, then into the matzo meal, ensuring a generous coating.

>5 Pour the oil into a non-stick frying pan to a depth of 1 cm/½ inch and heat. Cook the fish pieces in batches for a few minutes, turning once, until golden and cooked through.

>6 For the chilli mayonnaise, put the chilli sauce and mayonnaise in a bowl and beat together until combined.

Transfer the fish to warmed plates and
serve with the chilli mayonnaise on the side.

spiced mackerel with tropical salsa

serves 4

ingredients
2 tsp ground coriander
2 tsp ground cumin
½ tsp ground turmeric
¼ tsp cayenne pepper
pinch of salt
8 mackerel fillets
flatbreads, to serve

salsa
1 small avocado
1 small mango
1 small onion, finely chopped
juice of 1 lime

>1 Preheat a ridged griddle pan. Mix together the coriander, cumin, turmeric, cayenne and salt.

>2 Cut deep slashes in the skin side of each mackerel fillet and rub the spices all over.

Serve the mackerel with the salsa spooned over, accompanied by flatbreads.

>3 For the salsa, halve, stone and peel the avocado and mango, then cut into fine dice. Mix with the onion and lime juice.

>4 Cook the mackerel in the preheated griddle pan for 6–8 minutes, turning once, until cooked through.

seared sesame salmon with pak choi

serves 4

ingredients

2.5-cm/1-inch piece fresh
  ginger
1 tbsp soy sauce

1 tsp sesame oil
4 skinless salmon fillets
2 tbsp sesame seeds
lime wedges, to serve

stir-fry

2 small pak choi
1 bunch spring onions
1 tbsp sunflower oil

1 tsp sesame oil
salt and pepper

> **1** Peel and finely grate the ginger and mix with the soy sauce and sesame oil in a shallow dish.

> **2** Add the salmon fillets, turning to coat evenly on both sides.

> **3** Sprinkle the salmon on one side with half the sesame seeds, then turn and sprinkle the other side with the remaining sesame seeds.

> **4** Cut the pak choi lengthways into quarters.

>5 Cut the spring onions into thick diagonal slices.

>6 Preheat a heavy-based frying pan. Add the salmon and cook for 3–4 minutes. Turn and cook for a further 3–4 minutes.

>7 Meanwhile, heat the sunflower and sesame oils in a wok, add the pak choi and spring onions and stir-fry for 2–3 minutes. Season to taste with salt and pepper.

>8 Divide the vegetables between warmed serving plates and place the salmon on top.

Serve immediately with lime wedges for squeezing over.

spicy thai seafood stew

serves 4

ingredients

200 g/7 oz squid, cleaned and
  tentacles discarded
500 g/1 lb 2 oz firm white fish
  fillets, preferably monkfish or
  halibut

1 tbsp corn oil
4 shallots, finely chopped
2 garlic cloves, finely chopped
2 tbsp Thai green curry paste
2 small lemon grass stems, finely
  chopped

1 tsp shrimp paste
500 ml/18 fl oz coconut milk
200 g/7 oz raw king prawns,
  peeled and deveined
12 live clams, scrubbed

8 fresh basil leaves, finely
  shredded, plus extra leaves
  to garnish
freshly cooked rice, to serve

>1 Using a sharp knife, cut the squid into thick rings and cut the fish into bite-sized chunks.

>2 Preheat a large wok, then add the oil and heat. Add the shallots, garlic and curry paste and stir-fry for 1–2 minutes.

>3 Add the lemon grass and shrimp paste, then stir in the coconut milk and bring to the boil.

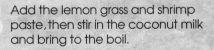

>4 Reduce the heat until the liquid is simmering gently, then add the squid, fish and prawns and simmer for 2 minutes.

Discard any clams with broken shells and any that refuse to close when tapped. Add the clams and simmer for a further minute, or until the clams have opened. Discard any that remain closed.

>6 Sprinkle the shredded basil leaves over the stew.

Transfer to serving plates, garnish with basil leaves and serve immediately with freshly cooked rice.

wine-steamed mussels

serves 4

ingredients

115 g/4 oz butter
1 shallot, chopped
3 garlic cloves, finely chopped
2 kg/4 lb 8 oz live mussels,
  scrubbed and debearded
225 ml/8 fl oz dry white wine
½ tsp salt
4 tbsp chopped fresh parsley
pepper
fresh crusty bread, to serve

> **1** Place half the butter in a large saucepan and melt over a low heat. Add the shallot and garlic and cook for 2 minutes.

> **2** Discard any mussels with broken shells and any that refuse to close when tapped. Add the mussels and wine to the pan with the salt and pepper to taste. Cover and bring to the boil, then cook for 3 minutes, shaking the pan from time to time.

Serve immediately with fresh crusty bread for mopping up the juices.

>3 Remove the mussels from the pan with a slotted spoon and place in individual serving bowls. Discard any mussels that remain closed.

>4 Stir the remaining butter and the parsley into the cooking juices in the pan. Bring to the boil, then pour over the mussels.

linguine with sardines

serves 4

ingredients

8 sardines, filleted, washed and
   dried
4 tbsp olive oil

3 garlic cloves, sliced
1 tsp chilli flakes
1 fennel bulb, trimmed and
   thinly sliced

350 g/12 oz dried linguine
½ tsp finely grated lemon rind
1 tbsp lemon juice
2 tbsp toasted pine kernels

2 tbsp chopped fresh parsley
salt and pepper

>1 Roughly chop the sardines into large pieces and reserve.

>2 Heat 2 tablespoons of the oil in a large frying pan over a medium–high heat and add the garlic and chilli flakes.

>3 Cook for 1 minute, then add the fennel. Cook, stirring occasionally, for 4–5 minutes, or until soft.

>4 Reduce the heat, add the sardine pieces and cook for a further 3–4 minutes.

> **5** Meanwhile, bring a large saucepan of lightly salted water to the boil. Add the pasta and cook for 8–10 minutes, or until tender but still firm to the bite.

> **6** Drain thoroughly and return to the pan.

> **7** Add the lemon rind, lemon juice, pine kernels and parsley to the sardine mixture and toss together. Season to taste with salt and pepper.

> **8** Add to the pasta with the remaining oil and toss together gently.

Transfer to a warmed serving dish and serve immediately.

hot-smoked salmon on hash browns

serves 4

ingredients

1 onion

800 g/1 lb 12 oz floury potatoes, peeled

2 tbsp chopped fresh dill, plus extra sprigs to garnish

1 tsp celery salt

25 g/1 oz butter

2 tbsp olive oil

1 bunch watercress

1 tbsp walnut oil

2 tbsp lemon juice

250 g/9 oz hot-smoked salmon, roughly flaked

pepper

lemon wedges, to serve

>1 Peel the onion, then grate the onion and potatoes in a food processor. Tip into a clean tea towel and squeeze out as much moisture as possible.

>2 Stir in the chopped dill and celery salt and season well with pepper. Divide into 8 portions.

>3 Heat half the butter and half the olive oil in a large frying pan. Add 4 heaps of the potato mixture and flatten lightly. Fry for 4–5 minutes, until golden underneath.

>4 Flip the hash browns over to cook on the other side until golden brown. Remove from the pan and keep warm whilst you repeat step 3 with the remaining mixture.

>5 Toss the watercress with the walnut oil and 1 tablespoon of the lemon juice. Divide between serving plates and place the hash browns on top.

>6 Top with the salmon and sprinkle with the remaining lemon juice and pepper to taste.

Garnish with dill sprigs and serve
with lemon wedges.

speedy tuna pizza

serves 4

ingredients

1 x 30-cm/12-inch
  ready-made pizza base
3 tbsp red pesto
200 g/7 oz canned tuna in
  sunflower oil, drained
175 g/6 oz cherry tomatoes,
  halved
100 g/3½ oz mozzarella
  cheese, diced
2 tbsp capers
8 small black olives, stoned
1 tbsp olive oil
salt and pepper

>1 Preheat the oven to 220°C/425°F/
Gas Mark 7. Place the pizza base on
a baking tray, then spread the pesto
evenly over the top.

>2 Roughly flake the tuna and arrange
over the pizza.

Serve the pizza hot
or cold.

> 3 Scatter over the tomatoes, mozzarella,
capers and olives. Season to taste with
salt and pepper.

> 4 Drizzle the oil over the pizza and bake in the
preheated oven for about 15 minutes, or
until golden and bubbling.

meat

paprika steak wraps with horseradish cream

serves 4

ingredients

4 sirloin steaks, about 175 g/
  6 oz each
1 garlic clove, crushed
2 tsp smoked paprika, plus
  extra for sprinkling
sunflower oil, for brushing
100 g/3½ oz crème fraîche
3 tbsp creamed horseradish
8 small flour tortillas
75 g/2¾ oz rocket leaves
2 firm, ripe avocados, peeled,
  stoned and sliced
1 red onion, thinly sliced
salt and pepper

> **1** Spread the steaks with the garlic and sprinkle both sides with the paprika. Season to taste with salt and pepper.

> **2** Preheat a ridged griddle pan to very hot and brush with oil. Add the steaks and cook for 6–8 minutes, turning once. Remove from the heat and leave to rest for 5 minutes.

Serve the wraps with a spoonful of horseradish cream, sprinkled with extra paprika.

> **3** Mix together the crème fraîche and horseradish, then spread half over the tortillas.

> **4** Slice the steaks into strips. Divide between the tortillas with the rocket, avocado and red onion, wrapping the sides over.

griddled steak with hot chilli salsa

serves 4

ingredients
sunflower oil, for brushing
4 sirloin steaks, about
    225 g/8 oz each
salt and pepper

hot chilli salsa
4 fresh red habanero chillies
4 fresh green poblano chillies
3 tomatoes, peeled, deseeded
    and diced
2 tbsp chopped fresh
    coriander

1 tbsp red wine vinegar
2 tbsp olive oil
salt

lamb's lettuce,
to garnish

>1 For the salsa, preheat the grill to high. Arrange the chillies on a foil-lined grill rack and cook under the preheated grill, turning frequently, until blackened and charred.

>2 Leave to cool. When cool enough to handle, peel off the skins.

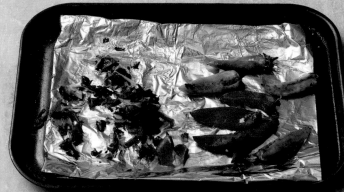

>3 Halve and deseed the chillies, then finely chop the flesh.

>4 Mix together the chillies, tomatoes and coriander in a bowl.

>5 Mix together the vinegar and olive oil in a jug. Season to taste with salt and pour over the salsa. Toss well, cover and chill until required.

>6 Heat a ridged griddle pan over a medium heat and brush lightly with sunflower oil. Season the steaks to taste with salt and pepper, and cook for 2–4 minutes on each side, or until cooked to your liking.

Serve immediately with the salsa, garnished with lamb's lettuce.

hot sesame beef

serves 4

ingredients

500 g/1 lb 2 oz fillet steak,
  cut into thin strips
1½ tbsp sesame seeds
125 ml/4 fl oz beef stock
2 tbsp soy sauce

2 tbsp grated fresh ginger
2 garlic cloves, finely chopped
1 tsp cornflour
½ tsp chilli flakes
3 tbsp sesame oil

1 large head of broccoli,
  cut into florets
1 yellow pepper, deseeded
  and thinly sliced
1 fresh red chilli, finely sliced

1 tbsp chilli oil, or to taste
salt and pepper
cooked wild rice, to serve
1 tbsp chopped fresh
  coriander, to garnish

> 1 Mix the beef strips with 1 tablespoon of the sesame seeds in a small bowl.

> 2 In a separate bowl, stir together the stock, soy sauce, ginger, garlic, cornflour and chilli flakes.

> 3 Heat 1 tablespoon of the sesame oil in a large wok. Stir-fry the beef strips for 2–3 minutes. Remove and set aside, then wipe the wok with kitchen paper.

> 4 Heat the remaining sesame oil in the wok, add the broccoli, yellow pepper, red chilli and chilli oil and stir-fry for 2–3 minutes.

>5 Stir in the stock mixture, cover and simmer for 2 minutes.

>6 Return the beef to the wok and simmer until the juices thicken, stirring occasionally. Cook for a further 1–2 minutes. Sprinkle with the remaining sesame seeds and season to taste with salt and pepper.

Serve over wild rice and garnish with fresh coriander.

orange & lemon crispy lamb cutlets

serves 2

ingredients
1 garlic clove, crushed
1 tbsp olive oil
2 tbsp finely grated orange rind
2 tbsp finely grated lemon rind
6 lamb cutlets
salt and pepper
orange wedges, to garnish

>1 Preheat a ridged griddle pan.

>2 Mix together the garlic, oil and citrus rinds in a bowl and season to taste with salt and pepper.

Garnish with the orange wedges and serve.

>3 Brush the mixture over the lamb cutlets.

>4 Cook the cutlets in the preheated griddle pan for 4–5 minutes on each side.

honeyed apricot lamb with lemon couscous

serves 4

ingredients

4 lamb leg steaks
4 tsp ground coriander
1 tbsp ground cumin
1 small butternut squash

1 tbsp olive oil
1 onion, chopped
600 ml/1 pint chicken stock
2 tbsp chopped fresh ginger

100 g/3½ oz ready-to-eat dried
 apricots
2 tbsp clear honey
finely grated rind and juice of
 1 lemon

200 g/7 oz couscous
salt and pepper
3 tbsp chopped fresh mint,
 to garnish

>1 Sprinkle the lamb steaks with the ground coriander and cumin.

>2 Peel and deseed the squash and cut into bite-sized chunks.

>3 Heat the oil in a flameproof casserole. Add the lamb and cook over a high heat for 2–3 minutes, turning once.

>4 Stir in the squash, onion and half the stock, then bring to the boil.

> **5** Add the ginger, apricots, honey and lemon juice and season to taste with salt and pepper. Cover and cook over a medium heat for about 20 minutes, stirring occasionally.

> **6** Meanwhile, bring the remaining stock to the boil in a small saucepan, then stir in the couscous and lemon rind with salt and pepper to taste. Remove from the heat, cover and leave to stand for 5 minutes.

Serve the lamb with the couscous, sprinkled with fresh mint.

pork in plum sauce

serves 4

ingredients

600 g/1 lb 5 oz pork fillet
2 tbsp groundnut oil
1 orange pepper, deseeded
   and sliced

1 bunch spring onions, sliced
250 g/9 oz oyster mushrooms,
   sliced
300 g/10½ oz fresh beansprouts
2 tbsp dry sherry

150 ml/5 fl oz plum sauce
250 g/9 oz medium egg
   noodles
salt and pepper

chopped fresh coriander,
   to garnish

>1 Slice the pork into long, thin strips.

>2 Heat the oil in a wok and stir-fry the pork for 2–3 minutes.

>3 Add the orange pepper and stir-fry for 2 minutes, then add the spring onions, mushrooms and beansprouts.

>4 Stir-fry for 2–3 minutes, then add the sherry and plum sauce and heat until boiling. Season well with salt and pepper.

>5 Meanwhile, cook the noodles in a saucepan of lightly salted boiling water for 4 minutes, until tender.

>6 Drain the noodles, then add to the wok and toss well.

122

Serve immediately, garnished with fresh coriander.

pork & rosemary burgers

serves 4

ingredients
500 g/1 lb 2 oz fresh pork mince
1 small onion, finely chopped
1 garlic clove, crushed
1 tbsp finely chopped fresh
  rosemary
oil, for brushing
1 small French baguette,
  split and cut into four
2 tomatoes, sliced
4 gherkins, sliced
4 tbsp Greek-style yogurt
2 tbsp chopped fresh mint
salt and pepper

>**1** Use your hands to mix together the pork, onion, garlic and rosemary with salt and pepper to taste.

>**2** Divide the mixture into four and shape into flat burger shapes.

124

Spoon the minty yogurt over the burgers and replace the baguette tops to serve.

>3 Brush a ridged griddle pan or frying pan with oil and cook the burgers for 6–8 minutes, turning once, until golden and cooked through.

>4 Place a burger on the bottom half of each piece of baguette and top with the tomatoes and gherkins. Mix together the yogurt and mint.

125

steamed chicken with chilli & coriander butter

serves 4

ingredients

55 g/2 oz butter, softened

1 fresh bird's eye chilli, deseeded and chopped

3 tbsp chopped fresh coriander

4 skinless, boneless chicken breasts, about 175 g/6 oz each

400 ml/14 fl oz coconut milk

350 ml/12 fl oz chicken stock

200 g/7 oz basmati rice

salt and pepper

pickled vegetables

1 carrot

½ cucumber

3 spring onions

2 tbsp rice vinegar

>1 Mix the butter with the chilli and coriander.

>2 Cut a deep slash into the side of each chicken breast to form a pocket.

>3 Spoon a quarter of the butter into each pocket and place on a 30-cm/12-inch square of baking paper.

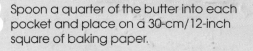

>4 Season to taste with salt and pepper, then bring two opposite sides of the paper together on top, folding over to seal firmly. Twist the ends to seal.

>5 Pour the coconut milk and stock into a large pan with a steamer top. Bring to the boil. Stir in the rice with a pinch of salt.

>6 Place the chicken parcels in the steamer top, cover and simmer for 15–18 minutes, stirring the rice once, until the rice is tender and the chicken is cooked through.

>7 Meanwhile, peel and trim the carrot, then cut the carrot, cucumber and spring onions into fine matchsticks. Place in a small bowl with the vinegar.

>8 Unwrap the chicken, reserving the juices, and cut in half diagonally.

Serve the chicken over the rice, with the juices spooned over and pickled vegetables on the side.

baked tapenade chicken

serves 4

ingredients

4 skinless, boneless chicken
  breasts
4 tbsp green olive tapenade

8 thin slices smoked pancetta
2 garlic cloves, chopped
250 g/9 oz cherry tomatoes,
  halved

100 ml/3½ fl oz dry white wine
2 tbsp olive oil
8 slices ciabatta
salt and pepper

>1 Preheat the oven to 220°C/425°F/ Gas Mark 7. Place the chicken breasts on a board and cut three deep slashes into each.

>2 Spread a tablespoon of the tapenade over each chicken breast, pushing it into the slashes with a palette knife.

>3 Wrap each chicken breast in two slices of pancetta.

>4 Place the chicken breasts in a shallow ovenproof dish and arrange the garlic and tomatoes around them.

>5 Season to taste with salt and pepper, then pour over the wine and 1 tablespoon of the oil.

>6 Bake in the preheated oven for about 20 minutes, until the juices run clear when the chicken is pierced with a skewer.

>7 Cover the dish loosely with foil and leave to stand for 5 minutes.

>8 Meanwhile, preheat the grill to high. Brush the ciabatta with the remaining oil and cook under the preheated grill for 2–3 minutes, turning once, until golden.

Transfer the chicken and tomatoes to serving plates and spoon over the juices. Serve with the toasted ciabatta.

chicken with creamy penne

serves 2

ingredients

200 g/7 oz dried penne
1 tbsp olive oil
2 skinless, boneless chicken
  breasts
4 tbsp dry white wine
115 g/4 oz frozen peas
5 tbsp double cream
salt
4–5 tbsp chopped fresh parsley,
  to garnish

>**1** Bring a large saucepan of lightly salted water to the boil. Add the pasta and cook for about 8–10 minutes, until tender but still firm to the bite.

>**2** Meanwhile, heat the oil in a frying pan, add the chicken and cook over a medium heat for about 4 minutes on each side.

Garnish with fresh parsley and serve.

>3 Pour in the wine and cook over a high heat until it has almost evaporated.

>4 Drain the pasta. Add the peas, cream and pasta to the frying pan and stir well. Cover and simmer for 2 minutes.

135

duck breasts with citrus glaze

serves 4

ingredients

55 g/2 oz light brown sugar,
  plus extra if needed
finely grated rind and juice of
  1 orange

finely grated rind and juice of
  1 large lemon
finely grated rind and juice of
  1 lime
4 duck breasts, skin on

2 tbsp olive oil
salt and pepper
freshly cooked sugar snap
  peas and orange wedges,
  to serve

>1 Put the sugar in a small saucepan, add just enough water to cover and heat gently until dissolved.

>2 Add the citrus rinds and juices and bring to the boil.

>3 Reduce the heat and simmer for about 10 minutes, until syrupy. Remove from the heat. Taste and add extra sugar if needed. Keep warm.

>4 Meanwhile, score the skin of the duck breasts with a sharp knife in a criss-cross pattern and rub with salt and pepper.

>5 Heat the oil in a frying pan. Place the duck breasts skin-side down in the pan and cook for 5 minutes on each side, until the flesh is just pink. Keep warm.

>6 Slice the duck breasts diagonally into 5–6 slices and transfer to warmed plates.

Arrange some sugar snap peas and
orange wedges on each plate, spoon over
the glaze and serve immediately.

turkey cutlets with parma ham & sage

serves 2

ingredients

2 skinless, boneless turkey cutlets

2 slices Parma ham, halved

4 fresh sage leaves

2 tbsp plain flour

2 tbsp olive oil

1 tbsp butter

salt and pepper

lemon wedges, to serve

>1 Slice each turkey cutlet in half horizontally into 2 thinner escalopes.

>2 Put each escalope between 2 sheets of clingfilm and pound lightly with a rolling pin. Season each escalope with salt and pepper to taste.

>3 Lay half a slice of ham on each escalope, put a sage leaf on top and secure with a cocktail stick.

>4 Mix the flour with salt and pepper to taste on a large plate. Dust both sides of each escalope with the seasoned flour.

>5 Heat the oil in a large frying pan, add the butter and cook until foaming. Add the escalopes and fry over a medium heat for 1½ minutes, sage-side down.

>6 Turn the escalopes over and fry for a further 30 seconds, or until golden brown and cooked through.

Serve immediately with lemon wedges for squeezing over.

creamy turkey & broccoli gnocchi

serves 4

ingredients
1 tbsp sunflower oil
500 g/1 lb 2 oz turkey stir-fry
  strips
2 small leeks, sliced diagonally
500 g/1 lb 2 oz ready-made
  fresh gnocchi
200 g/7 oz broccoli, cut into
  bite-sized pieces
85 g/3 oz crème fraîche
1 tbsp wholegrain mustard
3 tbsp orange juice
salt and pepper
3 tbsp toasted pine kernels,
  to serve

>1 Heat the oil in a wok or large frying pan,
then add the turkey and leeks and stir-fry
over a high heat for 5–6 minutes.

>2 Meanwhile, bring a saucepan of lightly
salted water to the boil. Add the gnocchi
and broccoli, then cook for 3–4 minutes.

Serve immediately, sprinkled with pine kernels.

>3 Drain the gnocchi and broccoli and stir into the turkey mixture.

>4 Mix together the crème fraîche, mustard and orange juice in a small bowl. Season to taste with salt and pepper, then stir into the wok. Gently warm through over a low heat.

desserts

blueberry amaretti mess

serves 4

ingredients
250 g/9 oz fresh blueberries
1 tsp almond extract
3 tbsp clear honey
70 g/2½ oz amaretti biscuits,
 plus extra to serve
400 g/14 oz Greek-style yogurt

>1 Place 200 g/7 oz of the blueberries in a bowl with the almond extract and 1 tablespoon of the honey. Mash lightly with a fork.

>2 Crumble the amaretti biscuits with your fingers to break up roughly.

Serve with extra amaretti
biscuits on the side.

>3 Lightly stir together the mashed berries,
biscuits and yogurt, then spoon into four
small glasses or dishes.

>4 Top with the remaining blueberries and drizzle
over the remaining honey.

pear & hazelnut pancakes

serves 4

ingredients

200 g/7 oz chocolate hazelnut
    spread

8 ready-made pancakes

4 ripe pears

40 g/1½ oz unsalted butter,
    melted

2 tbsp demerara sugar

55 g/2 oz toasted chopped
    hazelnuts, to serve

>1 Preheat the grill to high. Warm the chocolate spread gently in a small saucepan until softened.

>2 Using a palette knife, spread each pancake with a little of the warmed chocolate spread.

>3 Peel, core and chop the pears. Arrange the pears over the chocolate spread, then bring the opposite sides of the pancakes over the filling to enclose it.

>4 Lightly brush an ovenproof dish with a little of the melted butter.

151

>5 Arrange the pancakes in the dish. Brush the pancakes with the remaining melted butter and sprinkle with the demerara sugar.

>6 Place the dish under the preheated grill and cook for 4–5 minutes, until bubbling and lightly browned.

Scatter the toasted hazelnuts over the
pancakes and serve hot.

white wine & honey syllabub

serves 4

ingredients

3 tbsp brandy

3 tbsp white wine

600 ml/1 pint double cream

6 tbsp clear honey

55 g/2 oz flaked almonds

> 1 Combine the brandy and wine in a bowl.

> 2 Pour the cream into a large bowl and whip until just thickened.

> 3 Add the honey to the cream and whip for about 15 seconds.

> 4 Pour the brandy and wine mixture in a continuous stream into the cream and honey mixture, whipping constantly, until the mixture forms soft peaks.

155

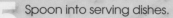

>5 Spoon into serving dishes.

>6 Transfer to the refrigerator and leave to chill for 2–3 hours.

Scatter over the flaked almonds and serve.

chocolate orange pots

serves 4

ingredients

1 orange
125 g/4½ oz plain chocolate,
  broken into pieces
30 g/1 oz unsalted butter
3 tbsp maple syrup
1 tbsp orange liqueur
125 g/4½ oz crème fraîche
strips of orange zest,
  to decorate

> **1** Cut the white pith and peel from the orange and lift out the segments, catching the juices in a bowl. Cut the segments into small chunks.

> **2** Place the chocolate, butter, maple syrup and liqueur in a small pan with the reserved orange juices and heat very gently, stirring, until smooth.

Scatter strips of orange zest over the top to serve.

> **>3** Stir in 4 tablespoons of the crème fraîche and the orange chunks.

> **>4** Spoon the mixture into serving dishes, then top each with a spoonful of the remaining crème fraîche.

quick tiramisù

serves 4

ingredients

225 g/8 oz mascarpone
   cheese
1 egg, separated

2 tbsp natural yogurt
2 tbsp caster sugar
2 tbsp dark rum
2 tbsp cold strong black coffee

8 sponge fingers
2 tbsp grated plain chocolate

>1 Put the mascarpone cheese, egg yolk and yogurt in a large bowl and beat together until smooth.

>2 Whip the egg white in a separate bowl until stiff but not dry.

>3 Add the sugar to the whipped egg white, then gently fold into the mascarpone mixture.

>4 Divide half the mixture between 4 sundae glasses.

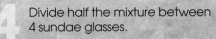

>5 Mix together the rum and coffee in a shallow dish.

>6 Dip the sponge fingers into the rum mixture, break them in half, or into smaller pieces if necessary, and divide between the glasses.

>7 Stir any remaining coffee mixture into the remaining mascarpone mixture and divide between the glasses.

>8 Sprinkle with the grated chocolate.

162

Serve immediately or cover and chill until required.

raspberry croissant puddings

serves 4

ingredients

30 g/1 oz unsalted butter,
  melted
4 croissants

225 g/8 oz fresh raspberries
4 tbsp maple syrup
350 ml/12 fl oz milk
2 large eggs, beaten

1 tsp vanilla extract
freshly grated nutmeg,
  for sprinkling

>1 Preheat the oven to 220°C/425°F/ Gas Mark 7. Place a baking tray on the middle shelf.

>2 Brush four 350-ml/12-fl oz ovenproof dishes with half the butter.

>3 Chop the croissants into bite-sized chunks. Mix with the raspberries and divide between the dishes.

>4 Spoon 1 tablespoon of the maple syrup over the contents of each dish.

> **5** Heat the milk until almost boiling, then quickly beat in the eggs and vanilla extract.

> **6** Pour the milk mixture evenly over the dishes, pressing the croissants down lightly.

> **7** Drizzle with the remaining butter and sprinkle a little nutmeg over each dish.

> **8** Place the dishes on the baking tray and bake in the preheated oven for about 20 minutes, until lightly set.

Serve hot.

brown sugar mocha cream dessert

serves 4

ingredients
300 ml/10 fl oz double cream
1 tsp vanilla extract
85 g/3 oz fresh wholemeal
  breadcrumbs
85 g/3 oz dark brown sugar
1 tbsp instant coffee granules
2 tbsp cocoa powder
grated chocolate, to decorate
  (optional)

>1 Whip together the cream and vanilla extract in a large bowl until thick and holding soft peaks.

>2 Mix together the breadcrumbs, sugar, coffee and cocoa powder in a separate large bowl.

Remove from the refrigerator and serve.

3

Layer the breadcrumb mixture with the whipped
cream in serving glasses, finishing with a layer
of whipped cream. Sprinkle with the grated
chocolate, if using.

Cover with clingfilm and chill in the
refrigerator for several hours, or overnight.

butterscotch, mango & ginger sundaes

serves 4

ingredients

100 g/3½ oz light muscovado sugar
100 g/3½ oz golden syrup

55 g/2 oz unsalted butter
100 ml/3½ fl oz double cream
½ tsp vanilla extract
1 large, ripe mango

115 g/4 oz ginger biscuits
1 litre/1¾ pints vanilla ice cream

2 tbsp roughly chopped almonds, toasted

> **1** To make the butterscotch sauce, melt the sugar, golden syrup and butter in a small pan and simmer for 3 minutes, stirring, until smooth.

> **2** Stir in the cream and vanilla extract, then remove from the heat.

> **3** Peel and stone the mango and cut into 1-cm/½-inch cubes.

> **4** Place the ginger biscuits in a polythene bag and crush lightly with a rolling pin.

>5 Place half the mango in four sundae glasses and top each with a scoop of the ice cream.

>6 Spoon over a little butterscotch sauce and sprinkle with the crushed biscuits. Repeat the layers.

>**1** Preheat the oven to 230°C/450°F/ Gas Mark 8. Mix the sultanas with the rum in a small bowl.

>**2** Place the cake slices, spaced well apart, on a baking tray.

>**3** Scatter a spoonful of the soaked sultanas over each slice.

>**4** Place a scoop of ice cream on top of each slice and place in the freezer until solid.

> **5** Meanwhile, whip the egg whites in a large bowl until soft peaks form.

> **6** Gradually whip the sugar into the egg whites, a tablespoonful at a time, until the mixture forms stiff peaks.

> **7** Remove the ice-cream-topped cake slices from the freezer and spoon the meringue over the ice cream, spreading to cover the ice cream completely.

> **8** Bake in the preheated oven for about 5 minutes, until starting to brown.

Serve immediately.

caramel pecan apples

serves 4

ingredients
55 g/2 oz unsalted butter
55 g/2 oz light muscovado
  sugar
4 crisp eating apples, cored
  and cut into wedges
1 tsp ground cinnamon
4 thick slices of brioche
4 tbsp rum or apple juice
30 g/1 oz pecan nuts

> **>1** Melt the butter in a sauté pan and stir in the sugar, apples and cinnamon.

> **>2** Cook over a medium heat, stirring occasionally, for 5–6 minutes, until caramelised and golden.

Spoon the apple mixture over the toasted brioche and serve immediately.

> **3** Meanwhile, toast the brioche on both sides until golden.

> **4** Stir the rum and pecan nuts into the pan and cook for a further minute.

warm honey muffins with strawberry salsa

serves 6

ingredients

butter or oil, for greasing
175 g/6 oz self-raising flour
1 tsp bicarbonate of soda
55 g/2 oz clear honey

40 g/1½ oz light muscovado
sugar
55 g/2 oz unsalted butter,
melted
1 egg, beaten

150 g/5½ oz Greek-style yogurt
finely grated rind of 1 small
orange
warmed honey, to glaze

salsa

200 g/7 oz fresh strawberries
2 tbsp clear honey
2 tbsp orange juice

>1 Preheat the oven to 200°C/400°F/Gas Mark 6. Lightly grease six 150-ml/5-fl oz individual metal tins or six cups in a deep muffin tin.

>2 Sift the flour and bicarbonate of soda into a bowl and add the honey, sugar, butter, egg, yogurt and orange rind, mixing lightly.

>3 Spoon the mixture into the tins and bake in the preheated oven for about 20 minutes, until risen, firm and golden.

>4 Meanwhile, for the salsa, hull and roughly chop the strawberries.

>5 Warm the honey and orange juice in a small pan, without boiling, then pour over the strawberries and stir lightly.

>6 Remove the muffins from the oven, lift carefully from the tins and brush the tops with honey to glaze.

Serve the muffins on warmed serving plates with a spoonful of strawberry salsa on the side.

plum & almond wraps

makes 4

ingredients

1 sheet (about 28 x 22-cm/
 11 x 8½-inch) ready-rolled
 puff pastry

30 g/1 oz ground almonds
30 g/1 oz golden caster sugar
½ tsp ground star anise
4 red plums

milk, for brushing

1
Preheat the oven to 220°C/425°F/Gas Mark 7.
Line a baking tray with baking paper. Cut the
pastry into four equal-sized rectangles, each
about 14 x 11 cm/5½ x 4¼ inches.

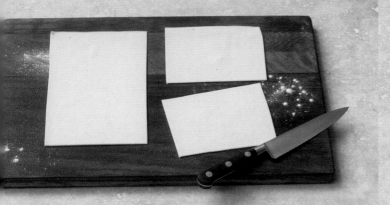

2
Stir together the ground almonds, sugar and
star anise, then place a tablespoonful in the
centre of each pastry rectangle.

3
Halve and stone the plums and
cut each into 8 slices.

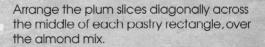

4
Arrange the plum slices diagonally across
the middle of each pastry rectangle, over
the almond mix.

>5 Sprinkle any remaining almond mix over the top, then fold two opposite corners of each pastry rectangle over to enclose the plum slices, securing with milk.

>6 Lift onto the baking tray and brush with milk to glaze. Bake in the preheated oven for 15–20 minutes, until firm and golden.

Serve the pastries warm.

no-bake chocolate fudge cake

serves 12

ingredients

225 g/8 oz plain chocolate,
  broken into pieces
225 g/8 oz unsalted butter
3 tbsp black coffee
55 g/2 oz light brown sugar
a few drops of vanilla extract
225 g/8 oz digestive biscuits,
  crushed
85 g/3 oz raisins
85 g/3 oz chopped walnuts

>**1** Line a 20-cm/8-inch round cake tin with baking paper.

>**2** Melt the chocolate and butter with the coffee, sugar and vanilla extract in a saucepan over a low heat.

Turn out and cut into thin slices to serve.

> **3** Stir in the crushed biscuits, raisins and walnuts and stir well.

> **4** Spoon the mixture into the prepared tin. Transfer to the refrigerator and leave to set for 1–2 hours.

Index